HALLOWEEN

Joseba Olivares

Editorial Vitalcode

Editorial: Vitalcode
Autor: Joseba Olivares

HALLOWEEN

Halloween is a holiday that is celebrated mainly on the night of October 31. Its origin goes back to ancient Celtic and Roman traditions, and it has evolved over the years into a mix of cultural and popular elements.

Halloween is characterized by its association with scary themes and the supernatural, such as ghosts, witches, monsters, and other creatures. During this holiday, people often decorate their homes with spooky items, wear costumes, and have themed parties. A common tradition is "trick or treating," in which costumed children go around neighboring houses asking for candy.

In addition to its playful side, Halloween also has deeper meanings. Some cultures believe that on this date the veil between the world of the living and the world of the dead becomes thinner, allowing communication with the spirits. It is also related to religious festivities such as All Saints' Day and the Day of the Dead.

www.ingramcontent.com/pod-product-compliance
Lightning Source LLC
Chambersburg PA
CBHW080852260726
48660CB00009B/3287